STEP-by-STEP

GEOGRAPHY

Farming and Industry

Patience Coster

Illustrated by Kate Aldous and

Andrew Farmer

W

FRANKLIN WATTS

NEW YORK • LONDON • SYDNEY

© 1997 Franklin Watts

First published in Great Britain by
Franklin Watts
96 Leonard Street
London
EC2A 4RH

Franklin Watts Australia
14 Mars Road
Lane Cove
NSW 2006
Australia

ISBN: 0 7496 2612 7
10 9 8 7 6 5 4 3 2 1
Dewey Decimal Classification 630
A CIP catalogue record for this book is available from the British Library

Printed in Dubai

Planning and production by The Creative Publishing Company
Design: Ian Winton
Consultant: Philip Steele

Photographs: Bruce Coleman: page 10 (Alain Compost), page 11 (Atlantide SDF),
page 15 (Brian J Coates); Hutchison Library: page 7 (Edward Parker), page 13, top, and page 18
(Sarah Errington), page 31, top (Tony Souter); Massey Ferguson Limited: cover; Tony Stone
Worldwide: page 5 (Mary Kate Denny), page 6 (Oliver Benn), page 13, centre (Gary John Norman),
page 17, top (John Garrett), bottom (Greg Probst), page 19 (James Strachan), page 21 (Michael
Rosenfeld), page 24 (Paul Chesley), page 27 (Walter Hodges), page 31, bottom
(Dennis O'Clair); ZEFA: page 8, page 9 (Engelbert), page 23.

Contents

Living on Earth   4

Basic Foods   6

Fruit and Vegetables   8

Other Harvests   10

Farming Animals   12

The Farming Year   14

Farming Then and Now   16

Feast or Famine   18

Making Things   20

Earth's Treasures   22

In the Factory   24

On the Move   26

Serving the Public   28

Caring for our World   30

Glossary   32

Index   32

Living on Earth

Have you ever thought about the different things you eat and use each day? What are they made of?

The children in this picture are having fun at a party. Look at all the things they are using.

Hat made from paper

T-shirt made of cotton

Juice from oranges

Ice-cream made from cows' milk

Plate made of china (pottery)

The food you eat may have been grown locally or far away in another country. It may then have been prepared in a factory or at a bakery. From there it will have been sent to the shop where you bought it.

Every day we use pens, books, clothes, tables and televisions. These things are made of different materials, such as plastic, paper, cotton and metal. Where do all these things come from? Have they been grown, or dug from the ground? Have they been made in factories?

Crisps made from potatoes

Bread made from wheat

Spoon made of steel

Tumbler made of plastic

Table made of wood

Basic Foods

We use the planet we live on to give us the food and materials we need. These people are harvesting a crop of potatoes.

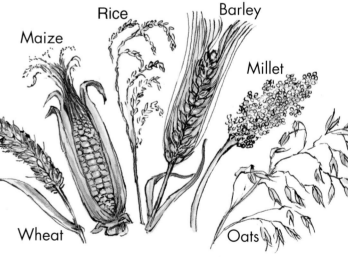

The most important foods are cereal crops. These are grains like wheat, maize, rice, barley, millet and oats.

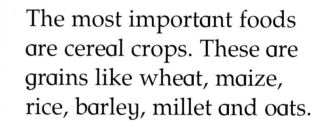

Rice is grown in wet fields in hot countries. It is the **staple food** of millions of people around the world.

Different grains are important in different parts of the world. In Africa and India, people use a lot of millet. In Central and South America, maize is more important. This Mexican farmer is tending his maize crop.

We use cereal crops to feed animals as well as people.

Different Types of Farming

Some farmers grow crops, others keep animals. On arable farms, the fields are used for crops. On pastoral farms, the fields are used as grazing land for animals. Mixed farms combine both arable and pastoral farming.

Fruit and Vegetables

We have to eat lots of different kinds of food to stay healthy. Fruit and vegetables provide us with many of the **vitamins** we need.

How many types of fruit can you see in this photograph?

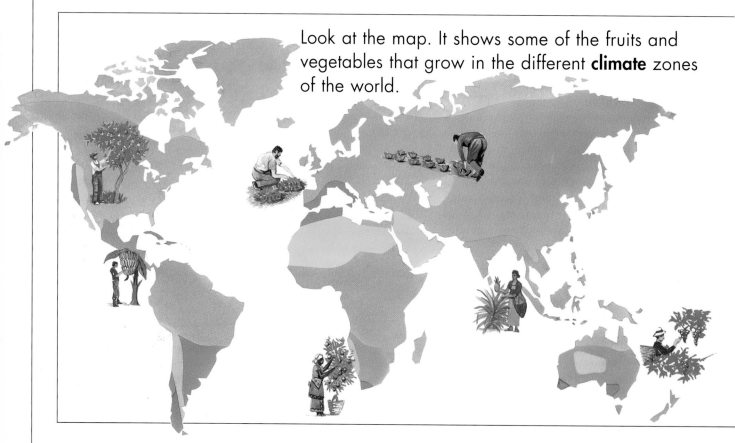

Look at the map. It shows some of the fruits and vegetables that grow in the different **climate** zones of the world.

GROW YOUR OWN BEANS!

1 Fill a plant pot with compost and push in four or five bean seeds. They should be about 2cm deep and 3cm apart. Cover the beans with a little compost.

2 Water, and cover the pot with newspaper.

3 When the beans sprout, uncover the pot and put it on a sunny windowsill. Keep it watered. The beans will need supporting with garden canes as they grow.

KEY

Arctic climate

Temperate climate
Apples, pears, cherries, raspberries, strawberries, plums, potatoes, carrots, onions and cabbages.

Mediterranean climate
Grapes, peaches, oranges, apricots, peppers, tomatoes, aubergines and olives.

Tropical/Monsoon climates
Bananas, pineapples, melons, dates, mangoes, yams, cassava, potatoes, soya beans, ground nuts and coconuts.

Hot/cold deserts

Growing Bananas

Bananas grow in hot countries. Bunches of bananas are picked when they are still green. These are then sent to the countries where they are to be sold. There they are ripened before being transported to the shops.

Other Harvests

Can you think of other things you and your family use every day? Tea is made from the leaves of bushes. This woman is picking tea in West Sumatra.

Coffee and chocolate are made from dried beans grown in hot countries. Sugar cane is also grown in hot countries. In cooler climates, a root crop called sugar beet is grown.

Wood and paper come from trees that have been cut down.

From Plants to Clothes

Cotton fibre is found in the seed heads of the cotton plant.

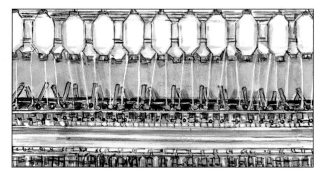

The cotton fibre is picked and then spun into thread.

Boats and ships search the seas for fish, an important and **nutritious** food source.

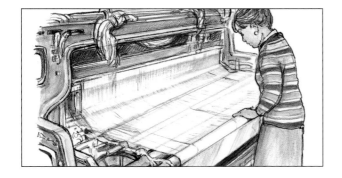

The thread is woven into a fabric.

The fabric is made into clothing.

Farming Animals

Farmers keep and breed animals for meat, wool or fur, skins and dairy products.

Sheep are farmed for meat and for their wool and milk.

Cattle provide meat. They give milk, which can be made into butter, cheese, cream and yoghurt. Their skins provide us with leather.

Goats are kept for meat and milk.

Pigs are farmed for meat.

Chickens, ducks and geese are kept for meat and for their eggs.

Turkeys are kept for their meat.

Some farmers keep just a few animals for their own needs. This is called subsistence farming.

Other farmers may look after thousands of animals on huge farms.

The Farming Year

An arable farmer's year is organized around planting, growing and harvesting crops. Around the world these things happen at different times, depending on the seasons.

Look at the picture. It shows the jobs the farmer has to do throughout the year.

1 Fertilizer is added to the soil and the ground is ploughed.

4 The harvest is gathered.

2 The seed is sown.

3 The crops are watered and sprayed to kill pests and weeds.

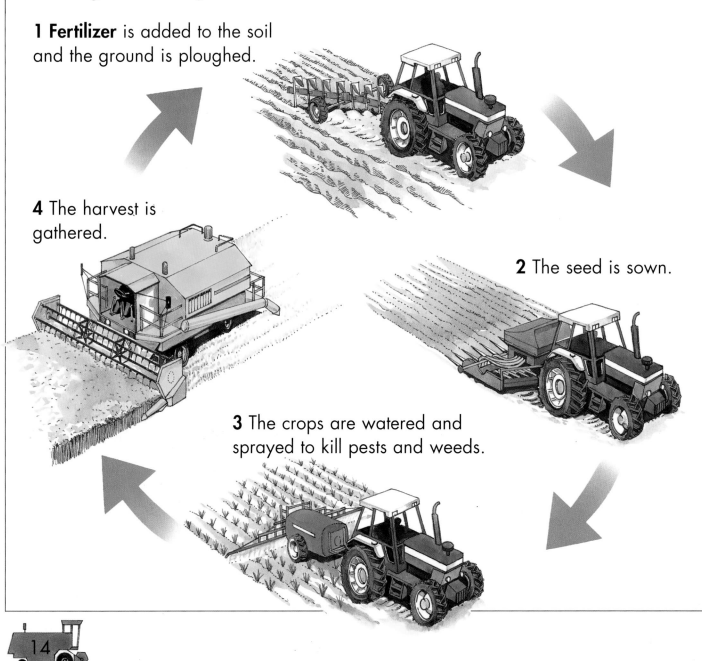

A pastoral farmer's year starts when their animals give birth. The pictures below show how a sheep farmer's year is organized.

In winter and early spring, the lambs are born.

In the summer, lambs are taken to market.

The farmer keeps some sheep for breeding. These are sheared in summer; the wool is sold.

Waiting for the Rains

In tropical countries, rice growers depend on a wind called the **monsoon**. This brings rain to water their crops. Farmers plant out small rice plants in the flooded fields.

In the autumn, the farmer buys female sheep for breeding.

Farming Then and Now

The first farmers lived in the Middle East around 10,000 years ago. They kept animals and cultivated the land.

In some parts of the world, farming has not changed for thousands of years. People still sow seeds by hand. They cut down the harvest with **scythes** or long knives.

In other parts of the world, farming has completely changed. Jobs like planting, sowing and harvesting are done by huge machines. Animals are fed and milked by machine, too.

Feast or Famine

In some parts of the world, the soil is not good for growing plants. If crops don't grow, people and animals go hungry. When crops fail, there may be terrible **famines**. Sometimes millions of people starve to death.

Droughts, plagues of pests and storms may also ruin the crops upon which people rely.

GROWING PLANTS IN DIFFERENT CONDITIONS

1 Take three seed trays and put sand into one, a mix of sand and soil into the second, and compost in the third. Sprinkle some poppy seeds into each tray.

2 Moisten the soil in trays two and three. Do not water the first tray.

3 After a few days, the seeds in trays two and three should have sprouted. Can you see any difference between them? The seeds in tray one will not have sprouted.

If rain doesn't fall for a long time, the soil turns to dust. It blows away, leaving the ground useless for farming. In hot, dry countries people build wells and use **irrigation systems** to water their crops. This photo shows irrigated land near the River Nile in Egypt.

In other parts of the world the soil and climate are better for growing crops. The farmers are richer and can afford chemicals to help crops grow and kill the insects that damage them. These regions produce more food than they can eat.

Making Things

When we grow or make things, we call it an industry. Farming is one kind of industry, but there are many others.

Long ago, Stone Age people learned to shape stones to make tools and weapons.

Later, people discovered how to use metals like bronze and iron.

They learned how to make pots from clay.

People still make things by hand today. This woman is weaving fabric on a machine called a loom.

This man is blowing glass through a metal pipe.

About 250 years ago, people began to build big factories to make lots of things more cheaply and quickly. Over the years, we have invented all kinds of machines to do the work for us.

Earth's Treasures

To make or build things, we use **raw materials** found in nature.

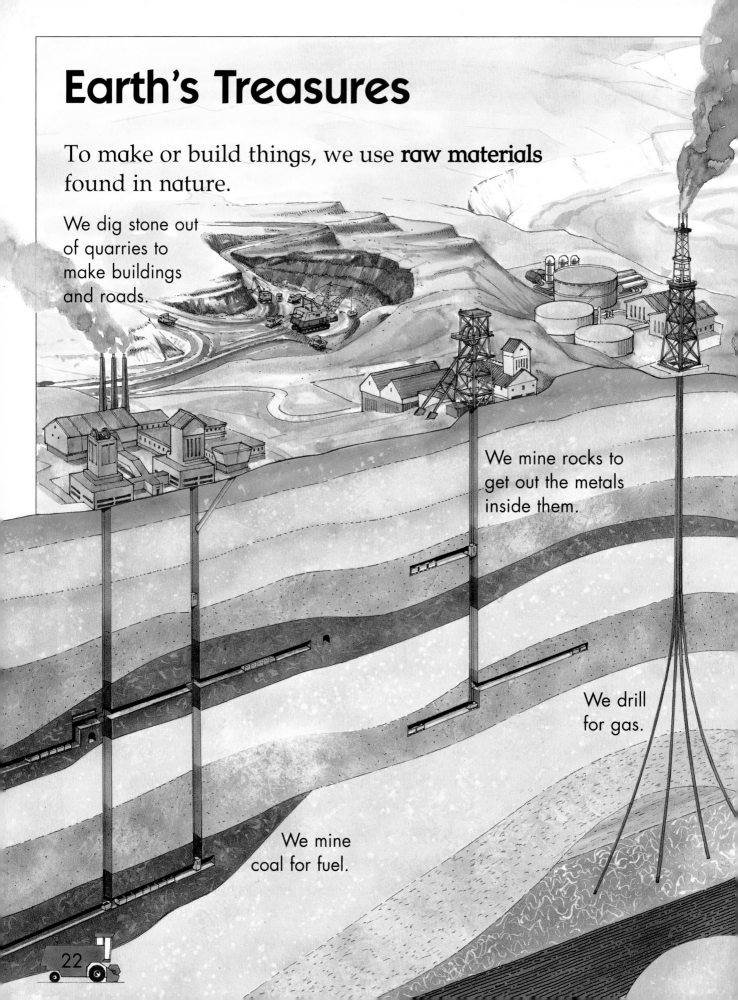

We dig stone out of quarries to make buildings and roads.

We mine rocks to get out the metals inside them.

We drill for gas.

We mine coal for fuel.

Energy and Industry

Most modern factories rely on **electricity** to run properly. Electricity powers machines, runs computers and provides lighting and heating. Coal, oil, **nuclear fuel** and gas are turned into electricity at power stations.

We drill for oil.

In the Factory

Around the world, different industries produce the things we buy and use in our daily lives. These women are inspecting cloth in a **textile mill** in Japan.

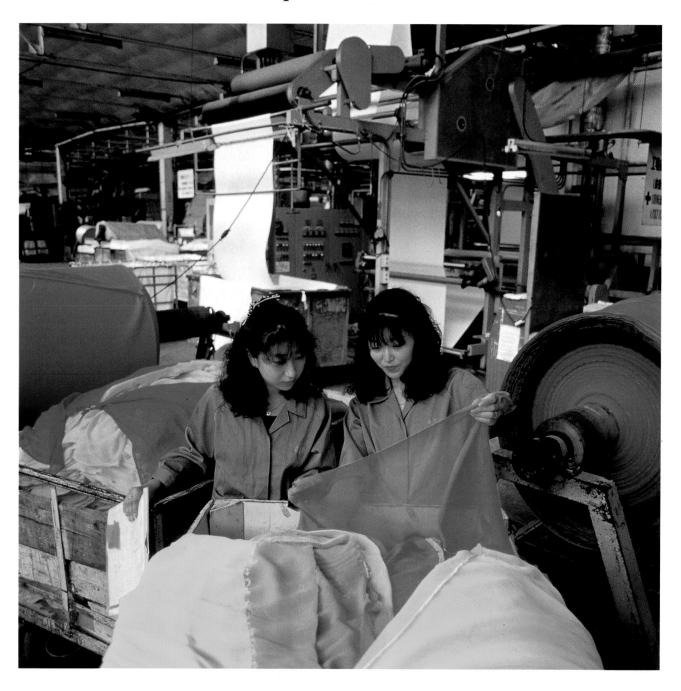

How a Chocolate Bar is Made

1 Cocoa beans are picked and dried, then shipped to the factory.

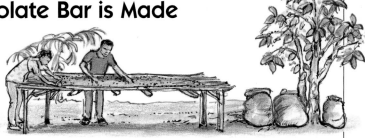

2 In the factory, the beans are roasted.

3 The beans are crushed and the shells are removed. Steel rollers grind them into a thick liquid to which sugar and milk are added.

4 The liquid is dried to a powder. Cocoa butter is added to make a paste, which is put into a machine and stirred slowly for six hours.

5 The paste is cooled and moulded into chocolate bars. These are wrapped in paper.

6 The chocolate bars are transported to the shops for you to eat.

On the Move

Industry relies on goods – and people – being transported from one place to another. Raw materials are taken to the factory so that things can be made. People travel to the factory to work. Goods are taken from the factory to the places where they will be sold.

Perishable goods, like many fruits and vegetables, need to be moved quickly. They are usually transported by road, or even by air.

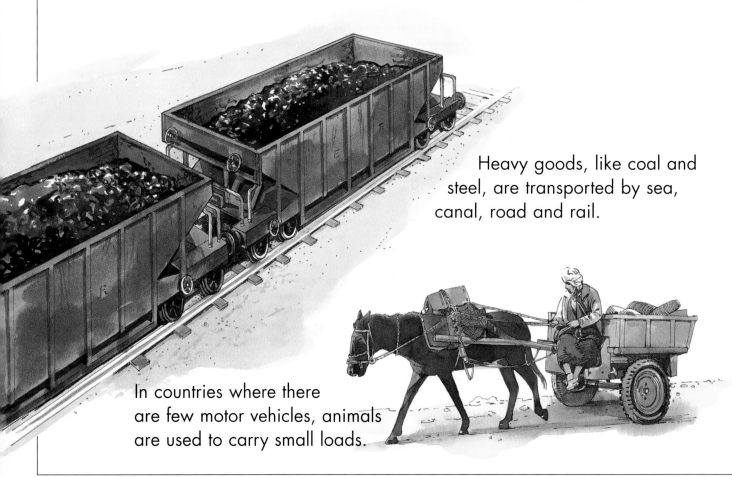

Heavy goods, like coal and steel, are transported by sea, canal, road and rail.

In countries where there are few motor vehicles, animals are used to carry small loads.

Liquids, like milk, are transported in special lorries.

Oil is transported by sea in huge tankers. On land it goes by road and pipeline.

Goods by Road

Huge lorries are used to transport goods in many parts of the world. They can carry loads of up to 50 tonnes.

Serving the Public

People don't just make things and grow things for a living. They work in offices, hotels, shops, hospitals, supermarkets and banks. They write for newspapers, make films and paint pictures. They empty rubbish bins and clean the streets. They are cooks and waiters in restaurants. All these people offer services to the public.

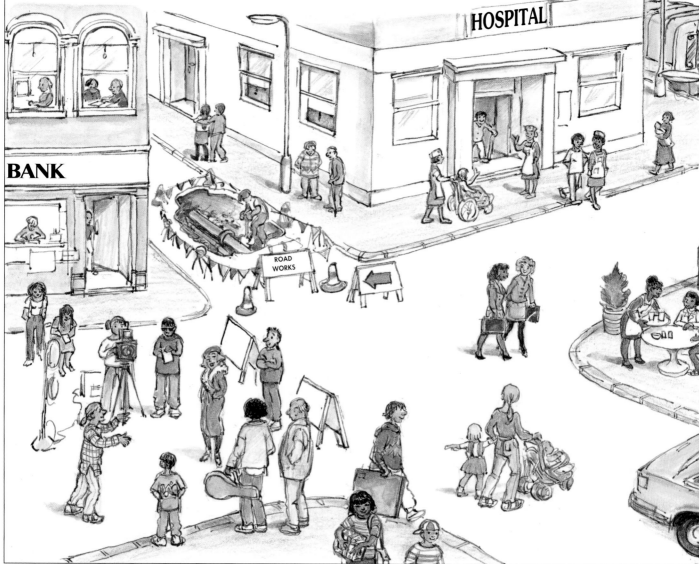

DAILY NEWS

CAFE

TAXI

MAKE YOUR OWN SHOP

1 Make some ice lollies by placing moulds containing fruit juice in the freezer overnight. Ask an adult to help you make a shop out of an old table. Decorate it with some brightly coloured paper.

2 Advertise the shop by making a sign to go outside your house. You can now sell ice lollies to all your friends. How much do you think you will charge for each one?

Caring for our World

Farming and industry can do a lot of damage to the **environment**.

If we grow too much in the soil without replacing the goodness, it becomes useless. If we use chemicals on farmland we might kill wildlife.

Waste from factories poisons the land, rivers and seas. Car **exhaust** fumes and smoking factory chimneys poison the air.

Scientists are trying to find out how to grow and make things without harming the planet we live on. Organic farmers raise crops and animals without using chemicals. Many industries now use **non-toxic** materials and are more careful about dumping waste.

Recycling for the Future

Many things can be used over and over again. Cans, bottles, jars, newspapers and magazines may all be taken to special bins for recycling. This way, you can help protect the Earth's resources.

Glossary

Climate: The sort of weather that is usual for a certain area over many years

Drought: Lack of rain

Electricity: A form of energy, used for lighting, heating etc.

Environment: Our natural surroundings, land, rivers, seas etc.

Exhaust: The used gases from a vehicle engine

Famine: Extreme shortage of food

Fertilizer: Substances put in the soil to improve plant growth

Irrigation systems: Systems that supply the land with water by means of man-made channels and ditches

Monsoon: A wind in South Asia, blowing from the south-west in summer and the north-east in winter

Non-toxic: Not poisonous

Nuclear fuel: Material, such as uranium and plutonium, used to make nuclear energy

Nutritious: Full of goodness

Perishable goods: Goods that decay fast

Raw materials: Materials in their natural state

Scythe: A tool with a long, single-edged blade using for cutting crops by hand

Staple food: The main food eaten in a certain area

Textile mill: A mill that produces cloth

Vitamins: Substances found in food that are important for human nutrition and growth

Index

Arable farming 7, 14

Bananas 9
Barley 6
Beans 9

Cattle 12-13
Cereal crops 6-7
Chemicals 19, 30-1
Chocolate 10, 25
Coffee 10
Cotton 5, 10-11

Electricity 23

Factories 4-5, 21, 23, 25, 26, 30-1
Famine 18
Fertilizer 14
Fishing 11
Fruit 8, 26

Gas 22-3
Glass 21
Goats 12

Irrigation 19

Maize 6-7
Metals 20
Milk 5
Millet 6, 27
Mining 22
Monsoon 15

Nuclear fuel 23

Oats 6
Oil 22-3, 27
Oranges 4
Organic farming 31

Pastoral farming 7, 15
Pigs 12
Plastic 4-5
Potatoes 5, 6
Pottery 4, 20
Poultry 12-13

Quarrying 22

Recycling 31
Rice 6, 15

Sheep 12, 15
Steel 5, 26
Subsistence farming 13
Sugar beet 10
Sugar cane 10

Tea 10
Textiles 21,. 24
Transport 26-7

Vegetables 8, 26

Wheat 5, 6
Wood 4, 10